A Feast of
French and Saunders

A Feast of French and Saunders

*Dawn French
and
Jennifer Saunders*

Heinemann : London

William Heinemann Ltd
Michelin House, 81 Fulham Road, London SW3 6RB
LONDON   MELBOURNE   AUCKLAND

First published 1991
Copyright © Dawn French and Jennifer Saunders 1991

A CIP catalogue record for this book
is held by the British Library
ISBN 0 434 27287 6

Phototypeset by Deltatype Ltd, Ellesmere Port, Cheshire
Printed in Great Britain by Clays Ltd, St Ives Plc

Contents

Introduction

We hope this lovely glossy volume will be seen, perhaps, as a representation of our very greatest work, or simply as a marvellous compilation of some of our funniest sketches, or at very least as a book of amazing quality that can raise a chuckle when read.

Each sketch itself represents real minutes of toil and labour, as well as hours of chocolate eating and magazine reading in the name of 'research'. The muse does not always come easily to us, and it can sometimes take in the region of a dozen Creme Eggs to bring it even close. A writer suffers.

It is, though, the finished product that matters and that is represented in this tome. So don't buy it thinking it will just be full of Creme Eggs because you will be very disappointed, and you won't get a penny from us.

We can guarantee that it will be snapped up and enjoyed by all our fans and any mildly interested human beings with a sense of humour. It is definitely not for those who hate us or are only interested in Dawn's bosoms.

It is difficult to remember quite when the idea of this book was broached, but the following transcript of our first lunch meeting with our publisher may throw light on that. (I tape all our meetings with publishers, they are wily folk who can talk you into a celebrity recipe book before you've even glanced at the menu.)

A bustling trendy London restaurant just downstairs from the publisher's office. Dawn and Jennifer sit opposite publisher. Lunchtime.

Publisher   (*Looking straight past Dawn and Jennifer and waving at Jane Asher on another table. Jane is ignoring her.*) How do you see this book?

Jennifer   Very much as a book. Pages and everything. We're not skimping, we don't just want a cover.

Publisher   I see. (*Makes note in Filofax.*) But may I get down to the nitty-gritty vis-à-vis the size factor of what we are calling in the office, for now – 'the book'. Are we talking 'pop-up stocking-filler coffee table with words'?

Dawn   I think you're talking hot stuff there! (*Thinks she's made a joke and laughs.*)

Jennifer   I think no. I think we're looking up-market. A classy number. I'm talking words, and a lot of them. Fabulously funny words, verbs, adjectives, the lot, the whole bloody alphabet in a glossy hardback with loose cover and no holds barred.

Publisher   Hold on there a moment. (*Writes furiously in Filofax.*) You're going too fast for me. They'll wet themselves in the office when they hear. We're talking a real book here. I don't think Lucy and Miranda have worked on a real book before. There'll be photocopying to do, memos, faxes, pestering phone calls, and of course lots of lunches.

Dawn   (*Between mouthfuls of truffles*) . . . and 'Capital Letters'.

Jennifer	Yes, lots of them.
Dawn	Fabulously funny ones.
Jennifer	We will include the very funniest material we've ever written.
Dawn	With hugely comical photographs.
Jennifer	If we can afford them.
Publisher	I'll clear that with Tom.

Dawn and **Jennifer**   Hurrah!

Publisher	(*On mobile phone.*) Fax main office, Lucy. We've got a real book on our hands. Capital letters and photographs. Take the dust cover off the photocopier. We're in business.
Dawn	Our public awaits. (*Too dramatic for her own good.*)
Jennifer	No longer will they have to sit pathetically hunched in front of their TV sets, desperately scribbling down our every gem.
Dawn	We will free them.
Publisher	(*Not one to waste a drinky moment.*) Champagne!
Dawn	Just a Baileys for me . . .

So there you have it, and perhaps this book, born of a lunchtime, can finally put to rest the rumour that our success is due only to fabulous make-up jobs, a good spot on BBC2 and a very close personal relationship with Sir Alan Yentob.

Sex Talk

Two chairs. Dawn sits on one and has her feet up on the other one. She is reluctant to vacate it. Jennifer edges closely and eventually Dawn submits and allows her to sit down.

Jennifer What are you doing this weekend?

Dawn I'm going riding in the country with my family, actually.

Jennifer Have you got a pony?

Dawn No, I've got a horse.

Jennifer How big is it?

Dawn You don't say 'how big is it' when you're talking about horses. You say, 'how many *hands* is it, please?'

Jennifer How many hands is it, please?

Dawn It's sixteen hands, thank you for asking.

Pause.

Jennifer Would you like to know what I'm doing this weekend?

Dawn No.

Pause.

Jennifer   I'm going to stay with my boyfriend.

Dawn   Oooh!! (*Long and sarcastic.*) Does your mum know?

Jennifer   Yeah . . . she doesn't know his parents are going away, though.

Dawn   OOOOOOOH!! (*Double the volume and sarcasm, sounds like a police siren now.*)

Long pause.

Jennifer   You know contraception?

Dawn   Yes.

Pause.

Jennifer   What is it, then?

Dawn   Well, if you're asking me about contraception, I bet you're going to *do it*. You're going to *do it*. You're going to *have it off*.

Jennifer is very embarrassed.

Dawn   Well, it's a good thing you've asked me because I know . . . The first thing you need for contraception is some towels. It's a good idea to use dark-coloured ones because they're going to get covered in a lot of muck and goo later on. You go up to the parents' bedroom, you take off the duvet and you spread the towels all over the bed. You get *on* the bed . . . and you have it off.

Jennifer   How do you know when you're having it off?

Dawn   God, you don't know anything, do you? Have you ever seen a man's toilet parts, or not?

Jennifer   Not.

Dawn   Right, well, a man has got three dangly toilet parts. And the (*she's checking in her mind*) . . . middle one is the important one. It's called 'his todger'. When the man wants to have it off, it stands up and gets all spikes sticking out of it, bit like a cactus. When it stands up, you know that it's time to get on the bed, open your legs and wait for the eggs to come.

Jennifer   Like a period?

Dawn   No, not like a period . . . Look, do you know about the four holes or not?

Jennifer   Not.

Dawn   Right. Well you've got four holes. Two in your back bottom and two in your front bottom. The two in your back bottom are for pooing and weeing, the two in your front bottom are for the period and the *eggs*. The egg starts to come down the front hole. It's about that big (*she indicates size of a football*), it's trying to get out but it can't because there's a bit of skin, it's just like a trampoline, it's called the hymen. The egg hits this and it keeps bouncing back up, it can't get out. By now, the todger's about this big (*indicates size to be three-feet long*) and there's a big metal spike coming out the end of it. And he puts it inside and tries to break the hymen by bashing and bashing and bashing into it until it breaks and a lot of green slime comes out of it. It's true. And that's when you know you're having an organism. The other way you know is because your eyes go like this. (*She looks up, only showing whites of eyes. Jennifer copies.*) Then the egg drops out on the carpet. You've got to wrap it in the towels, and put it in the toilet. You'll never believe what happens next. I couldn't believe it myself when I first saw it. By now the todger is this big (*arms fully outstretched*). The man stands up and says 'Oh God, oh God,' and the top of the todger opens up, and five thousand million trillion fish come jumping out. They bounce off the ceiling, off the walls, everywhere. You've got to scrape them into a towel and put them in the toilet. You mustn't let the fish get near the egg because that's when you get pregnant.

Jennifer   Do the fish just die then?

Dawn   Most of them do, if there's any left over, flapping around on the floor (*demonstrates fish flaps*), you just get them by the tails, you get a big hammer or a mallet and you bash them, bash them on the head until they're dead. Then you scrape them into a towel and put them in the toilet. (*Pause.*) Very pleasurable experience. Don't get pregnant though.

Jennifer   I don't want to get pregnant.

Dawn   Do you know about having babies or not?

Pause.

Jennifer   Not.

Dawn   Well, you get a lot of pain in your tummy and you

have to go to hospital in an ambulance. When you get there, the doctor comes to look up you with all his friends. He says, 'Oh no, the hole's not big enough.' So they get a big sledge-hammer and bash and bash your leg bones until they're pointing backwards. (*Demonstrates.*) A lot of people think babies come out forwards, but they don't, they come out sideways, you know. So he stands there holding you together, saying 'Here comes the baby!!' Eventually, he opens up the flap and the baby plops out with all the blubber . . . which you've got to *eat*!! Then they put your legs in plaster of Paris and you spend the rest of your life in a wheelchair. It's a very natural and beautiful experience.

Jennifer   I see.

Dawn   Don't be scared though. You have a lovely time with your boyfriend this weekend.

Jennifer   (*Faltering.*) I will, thanks.

Fashion Expert

*TV AM set – large sofa. Jennifer is the interviewer,
Dawn the 'expert'.*

Jennifer So, today I'm joined by Dawn French, top fashion
expert to the stars and the high street. So tell me,
Dawn, what can we expect to see in the shops this
year?

Dawn Clothes, mostly . . . and some hats and some shoes.

Jennifer I see, so what's really '*in*' this year?

Dawn Fabric is 'in', we'll be seeing jackets, skirts,
trousers, blouses, bras, underwear, maxis, minis,
midis, etc., tops and coats in fabric and certain
textiles.

Jennifer So anything goes fabric-wise. And what about this
year's colours? Purple?

Dawn Yes.

Jennifer Green?

Dawn Yes.

Jennifer Yellow?

Dawn Yes, and red and brown.

Jennifer Ah, so *not* blue then?

Dawn   Yes, blue . . . and black or white . . . and lilac.

Jennifer And shapes?

Dawn   Well, some shapes I know are circles, squares, rectangles, triangles.

Jennifer Dodecahedrons?

Dawn   Inevitably, there will some, yes.

Jennifer Hats?

Dawn   Do you mean for the head?

Jennifer Yes, indeed.

Dawn   Only if you want to wear them, you don't *have* to. We at the top of the fashion business are leaving it up to the people to decide if they want to wear a hat or not.

Jennifer Of course it depends if one is inside or outside. And have we got time for a fashion tip? – Yes, I think we have.

Dawn   Right, a fashion tip, always carry one of these in case of rain. (*Takes out piece of plastic.*) You put it on your head, or anywhere rain might land, you see!

Jennifer So, to sum up . . . what can we expect to see on the catwalk?

Dawn   Some cats.

Jennifer Thank you very much. Illuminating as always.

Mother and Daughter

Inside the living room of a suburban house.
Voice from hallway.

Mother Get in there now, madam. Not upstairs, in the front room.

Daughter (Jennifer) dressed in leather jacket carrying plastic carrier bag, slouches into the living room. Mother (Dawn) follows, looking severe.

Mother Sit down. (*Daughter sits.*) What is the matter with you?

Daughter Nothing.

Mother What do you mean, nothing?

Daughter Nothing!

Pause. Mother staring at Daughter.

Daughter It's just I didn't want to buy these jeans.

Mother What is the matter with these jeans?

Daughter I just didn't want to buy these ones, that's all.

Mother Well, which ones did you want then?

Daughter Why can't I just have the falmers ones like everybody has?

Mother What is the difference between the falders . . .

Daughter Falmers.

Mother . . . falders jeans and those ones?

Daughter It's just everyone else has the . . .

Mother Oh! Everyone else has the others. You can't be individual, can you? Got to be like everybody else.

Daughter It's not that.

Mother Well if you'd told me I could have got Aunty Mae to run you up a pair of falders . . .

Daughter She can't make jeans.

Mother She can make jeans, she was a tailoress in the war.

Pause.

Daughter Why can't I just go to the shop and buy them?

Mother Yes, why can't you just go to the shop and buy them? (*Pause.*) With what?

Daughter My money.

Mother With whose money, sorry?

Daughter (*Quietly.*) Your money.

Mother Yes, my money for which I work how hard?

Daughter Very hard.

Mother Yes, very hard. Five pounds ninety-nine pence those jeans cost. And don't you forget it.

Pause. Mother looks hard at Daughter. Daughter trying to look away.

Daughter   What you looking at . . . Stop looking at me.

Mother   I think it's about time we had a little talk, don't you?

Daughter   What about?

Mother   I was in your bedroom the other day. I was appalled at the mess.

Daughter   My bedroom.

Mother   Crunchy underwear all over the floor.

Daughter   It's my bedroom.

Mother   Yes, it may be your bedroom but it's my house, madam. While I was in your bedroom I noticed certain reading matter on your bedside table.

Daughter looks horrified.

Daughter   It's not my book. It's for school.

Mother   Oh, it's for school, is it? You're reading *Chopper* for school, are you? Well, maybe I should ring up your teacher and ask her, should I?

Daughter shakes head.

Mother   Yes, well I'm glad it's not your book because I've burned it.

Daughter   You can't burn other people's books.

Mother   I can burn anything I like, madam, if it's in my

house. I could burn the carpets, the curtains . . .
Also, while I was in your bedroom, I happened to
come across, (I wasn't looking), I just happened to
come across your diary . . .

Daughter indignant.

Daughter You can't read my diary . . .

Mother I wasn't looking.

Daughter My property. That's my property.

Mother Where were you last Tuesday night?

Daughter Ballroom dancing . . .

Mother Don't lie to me. You weren't, were you! Mrs
Wood was on the bus and saw you going into a
pub with a boy in a leather jacket.

Daughter Wasn't me.

Mother It was you. (*Mother softens.*) Who is the boy?

Daughter Nobody.

Mother What's his name?

Daughter Nobody. It's nobody.

Mother Well, I think Daddy and I would like to meet Mr
Nobody. Why don't you bring Mr Nobody home
for tea?

Daughter (*Muttering under breath.*) Stupid. You're so stupid.

Mother . . . Bring him home for tea so Daddy and I can
meet him.

Daughter   You won't like him, you never like any of my friends.

Mother   (*Pause.*) You know what I don't like. I don't like your attitude, madam. (*Notices something in Daughter's pocket.*) What is that in your pocket?

Daughter tries to hide something in pocket.

Mother   What is that in your pocket?

Daughter   It's nothing.

Mother   Put it in my hand now.

Daughter   It's nothing.

Mother   I'm counting up to ten. One, two, three . . .

Daughter pulls cigarette packet out of pocket. Hands it to Mother.

Mother   (*Horrified.*) What are these? (*Daughter doesn't react.*) What are these?

Daughter   What does it look like?

Mother   Don't push it. What are these?

Daughter   Cigarettes.

Mother   Yes, I can see that for myself, thank you. Have you been smoking these?

Daughter   No, I haven't.

Mother   Yes, you have. I can smell it on your breath.

Pause.

Why didn't you tell me?

Daughter You didn't ask.

Mother Don't push it. You lied to me. (*Begins to cry.*)

Daughter I didn't lie.

Mother It'll be heroin next.

Daughter Don't be stupid.

Mother Well. You've betrayed me and I'm going to have to tell your father about it.

Daughter Oh please don't, don't tell him.

Mother Don't grovel. It's just humiliating. Right you can get upstairs now and tidy your room.

Daughter I've got to go out.

Mother You are not going out for two weeks, madam.

Daughter I've got to go out . . . for school . . .

Mother And while you're about it you can clean out that rabbit. How would you like to live knee-high in your own droppings? Huh?

Daughter Wouldn't.

Mother Well, neither does he. So just buck up and *do* something about yourself.

Mother goes to leave.

Daughter (*Quietly.*) Mum, sorry.

Mother What?

Daughter Nothing.

West Country

Kitchen of a small country house. Large pine table, Aga, lots of old pans and dried flowers: looks more like an antique shop display than a working kitchen. Jennifer has a pile of ironing. Dawn enters, crosses over to Jennifer. They talk. The table and ironing board are out. They are wearing cleaners' nylon overalls.

Dawn　　Morning, Kath.

Jennifer　Morning.

Dawn　　You all right?

Jennifer　Yeah, how are you, my dear?

Dawn　　Very well. Is that all right with you, changing these days over for working here?

Jennifer　Yeah.

Dawn　　You're doing Thursday, Fridays.

Jennifer　Fine by me.

Dawn　　I do Monday, Tuesday, Wednesdays now. That's OK is it?

Jennifer　That's fine.

Dawn　　It's just that I've got to pick up my kiddies on

Thursdays, Fridays and those are Bob's days for
gettin' pissed down the pub lunchtimes.

Jennifer   That's fine by me, yeah.

Dawn   Got to do all that today? (*Pointing at pile of ironing.*)

Jennifer   No, well, old 'fart ass' isn't down till the weekend,
is she?

Dawn   Oh, she's coming this weekend, is she?

Jennifer   This weekend, yes.

Dawn   Oh, right. Do you want a cup of tea?

Dawn moves over to work-top by sink.

Jennifer   All right then, yeah, lovely.

Dawn   Oh, I don't want any of this herbal muck she's got
here, rosemary or tuna fish and the like. Get that
PG Tips.

Jennifer   Where's that?

Dawn   Top left-hand drawer of that dresser over there.

Jennifer   Yeah.

Dawn   That's where I keeps it, she makes me hide it again
from her friends.

Jennifer   Oh, her friends!

Dawn   Oh, I know, did you see the ones that was down last
weekend?

Jennifer   Oh yes, my goodness.

Dawn   She gets the old cream teas out – doesn't she, for
them?

Jennifer   That's right, that's right. Yeah.

Dawn   And they sit there stuffing their faces and saying, 'Ooh, I am so naughty.'

Jennifer   Yeah, 'I mustn't have any more.'

Dawn moves with cups of tea from work-top to table and sits down.

Dawn   'Oh, don't tempt me, Alexandra!'

Jennifer   You'd think they were having it off with the cream tea, not just eating it, wouldn't ya?

Dawn   Yeah, couldn't believe it!

Jennifer picks up T-shirt from draining board of sink.

Jennifer   Do you see this T-shirt? How much you reckons she paid for it?

Dawn   What? A T-shirt?

Jennifer   Yeah.

Dawn   Three quid tops.

Jennifer   Forty quid.

Dawn   Forty quid!

Jennifer   Forty quid, for this, you know how I know?

Dawn   How?

Jennifer   'Cos I put it in the washer and it's dryclean apparently.
Dawn   No.

Jennifer   Forty quid I paid for that, she says.

Dawn   No, no.

Jennifer   A T-shirt dryclean, I couldn't believe it.

Dawn   Money to burn, surprised she doesn't dryclean her knickers next.

Jennifer   Yeah. Here, do you want some poison?

Dawn   What?

Jennifer   Do you want some of this poison? (*Jennifer comes over to table to cut bread.*)

Dawn   Oh that's right, init, yeah.

Jennifer   White bread is poison, that's the thing.

Dawn   Yeah, white bread's poison unless of course it's French and is shaped like a penis. And then she stuffs it down her throat saying, 'It's heaven,' then, 'Ooh, it's heavenly.'

Jennifer   Yeah, it's 'darling bread', init, absolutely lovely 'darling bread'.

As Jennifer is saying speech she moves to fridge to get butter and ham and brings back to table.

Jennifer   Oh, you know what I had to do, I had to throw out all those joints. Only ham left.

Dawn   Yeah.

Jennifer   No meat anymore, remember?

Dawn   I know. That's right, no meat, init. I made her a cup of tea the other day, I said 'Don't worry, my lover, hasn't got any *meat* in it.'

Jennifer   Yeah, she drinks that coffee with no coffee in it. Tea with no tea in it.

Dawn   Sugar kills ya! Yes, sugar kills you. Fact that my old mother's been drinking sugar in her tea for the last eighty-seven years and she's perfectly all right doesn't matter.

Jennifer   No.

Dawn   No. Oh, her 'fart-ass' majesty! It's all right for her to stick half a ton of cocaine up her nostrils, but don't have sugar in your tea.

Jennifer sits down at table.

Jennifer   That's right, absolutely. Here, I tell you a thing the other day, right. After what you told me. I went down our barn, I took out all the old tools, we had, right.

Dawn   Yeah.

Jennifer   Like the gintraps and like the shovels and the saucepans and that, the old things we were going to chuck out. She paid fifty quid for 'em!

Dawn   (*Disbelief.*) No.

Jennifer   Fifty quid for 'em!

Dawn   No.

Jennifer   Couldn't believe it.

Dawn   No.

Jennifer   She just did it – 'I'll have those for fifty quid.'

Dawn   What's she doing with them then?

Jennifer Oh, don't you know?

Dawn No.

Jennifer Don't you know – have you seen over here? Look at this.

Jennifer moves to get gintrap off shelf and shows it to Dawn.

Jennifer That's our old gintrap, that is.

Dawn Look what she's done.

Jennifer Yeah, she's painted it, stencilled it apparently.

Dawn What's that stuck in it?

Jennifer That's dried flowers.

Dawn No! What does she do with those then?

Jennifer She gives them away as gifts apparently to her friends. Poor buggers.

Dawn Oh lord.

Jennifer She's crackers, isn't she?

Jennifer comes back and sits at table.

Dawn You know what she did the other day, I thought she'd completely flipped, she came round my house and she wanted to buy our old privy out of our back yard.

Jennifer Oh yeah, what for?

Dawn Yeah, well she asked me, she said, isn't it lovely that old privy, and I said well four generations of my

family had shat on it. Then she cried, and she
offered a hundred-and-fifty quid for it.

Jennifer A hundred-and-fifty quid.

Dawn I know, couldn't believe it! She wants to put pansies
in it apparently.

Jennifer Oh right.

Dawn Might clear the stink.

Jennifer Oh yeah, like what she did with old Geoff's boots.
Have you seen them?

Dawn No.

Jennifer She bought a pair of old Geoff's wellies for twenty
quid.

Dawn Yeah.

Jennifer Filled 'em with earth and put pansies in them in the
porch.

Dawn Oh, I've seen that, couldn't believe it. Well, I saw
her doing it actually – yeah, she had mud up to her
elbows.

Jennifer Well, she likes that, a bit of mud makes her feel like
she's in the country. Come down at weekends have
a bit of a walk in the old dingle. Didn't she? And
complain about the barbed wire again. Then off in
her Suzuki jeep back up to London.

Dawn Oh, don't mention that blessed jeep.

Jennifer What's that?

Dawn Oh, don't talk to me about that. Bloody sewing

	machine on wheels Bob calls it. You heard what happened the other day?
Jennifer	What's that?
Dawn	She's coming down our drive, right, she was coming to bring my mother a quiche. Have you heard about that?
Jennifer	What's that?
Dawn	Bacon egg pie, that's all it is.
Jennifer	Oh, I know what that is.
Dawn	And the Suzuki jeep went down a pot-hole. Got stuck. We had to tow her out.
Jennifer	Did you charge her for that?
Dawn	Yeah, a hundred quid we charged her.
Jennifer	Oh.
Dawn	She paid it, she paid it.
Jennifer	Did you have to borrow a tractor or something?
Dawn	No, Bob did it with his Mini.
Jennifer	Did he?
Dawn	Yeah.
Jennifer	That's good, init.
Dawn	She was coming down our house with her tape recorder to see my mother.
Jennifer	Oh yes.
Dawn	Have you heard about this?

Lanananeeneenoonoo. With the lovely Kathy Burke.

'Elvis lives!' – no, it's just us again.
With the lovely Stephanie Beecham.

We thought we
looked really like
them!

1980. The Comic
Strip. Desperate
for fame but
destined for a few
more years of
obscurity.

An excuse to dress up and look silly.

Another excuse to dress up and look silly.

With padding!!

Our tribute to Elizabethan times. Note that Dawn is wearing her 'satsuma on a rope'. Historically correct.

'Can't we get Charles Dance to do something?'

An Elizabethan beauty. Historical fact.

The Extras. 'It must have been much harder
to shave in Jewish times.'

Asking the lovely June Whitfield from
Terry and June for Paul Eddington's autograph.

With the lovely
Toyah Wilcox.

Extras in *Carmen*, the
opera.
'We would be drunk,
wouldn't we?'

'Just rusks for the Queen Mum, I'm afraid.'

'We're not trying to make a point, we're not trying to say anything.'

Jennifer	Yeah.
Dawn	She wants my mother to tell her stories about the village or oral history, she calls it.
Jennifer	Is that about your teeth or something?
Dawn	No, no, no. It's like she wants interesting stories of old about the village.
Jennifer	Oh yeah.
Dawn	Well, my mum don't know any. So I told her to tell her like, you know, Black Bess was born in our barn, something like that.
Jennifer	She paying 'er for that?
Dawn	No, she says she wants to buy my mother a gift instead of paying her.
Jennifer	I won't depress you but look forward to the return of your privy all painted up with ducks and primroses and stuffed with dried flowers. Oh dear, I think that's what she's doing out the back.
Dawn	Oh Kath!
Jennifer	Yeah.
Dawn	Something I meant to tell you, got the diary?

Jennifer fetches diary.

Dawn	Is it free next week, this place?
Jennifer	Let's have a look, yes, it's free next week.
Dawn	She's not coming down?
Jennifer	No.

Dawn	No, 'cos you know that advert I had in the *Observer*?
Jennifer	Yeah.
Dawn	Well, I've had a response.
Jennifer	Oh good.
Dawn	A young couple from Hammersmith wants to come down. So long as they're gone by Friday lunchtime she's none the wiser and I've got two hundred quid to spend up Asda.
Jennifer	That's good. The one thing I meant to tell you, right.
Dawn	Yeah.
Jennifer	Yesterday BBC was round here. BBC people came down. They're looking for a location apparently for *Miss Marple*.
Dawn	Oh, I love that.
Jennifer	I love that, yeah! Locations are gorgeous and they want it for the whole of May. They want this place here. A typical cottage they thought it were, right. I offered them my place but they weren't happy with the double glazing and the satellite dish. They want this place, so what we gonna do?
Dawn	Got to keep her away, haven't we?
Jennifer	Yeah.
Dawn	Well it's all right the first two weeks of May. She's in Bangladesh to get some rugs for the front room.
Jennifer	Oh right.
Dawn	Now, what we gonna do about the second two

weeks? I know, I tell her it's annual pig-slaughtering fortnight in the villages, that we's usually have to drink the blood or something.

Jennifer Oh right, yeah.

Dawn That'all keep her, she won't come down then.

Jennifer That'all keep her away. That's good, init. The one thing is, they want to paint it pink and put a thatch on it. That be all right, won't it?

Dawn Umm.

Jennifer She might not even know.

Dawn Well if she notices, right, you ever see *Witness*, the film? . . . Well, I'll tell her that Armish men folk of the village have done it as a harvest and festival gift for her.

Jennifer Oh all right then.

Dawn That'all be good.

Jennifer OK, my dear.

Dawn How much we getting for that?

Jennifer Well if it comes off, it'all be ten grand.

Dawn Oh!! We split that then, Kath.

Jennifer All right, fifty–fifty.

Dawn Fifty–fifty.

Points of View

Inside a living room. A Mother and two daughters (Jennifer and Dawn) are watching TV. We do not see the TV screen. The Mother speaks like the voices that read out the letters on Points of View.

Mother   That is never a new-born baby! (*Pause.*) There is absolutely no need for us to have to watch a grown woman with teeth like that . . . and she's supposed to be the pretty one! . . . Is she his wife? Or is that the other one?

Jennifer   We don't know, Mum, because you talked over the important part.

Pause.

Mother   Oh, look at that. A seventeenth-century pit pony wearing a modern snaffle bridle, . . . I don't think so! (*Pause.*) I'm not an expert but even I know that those would never have been used in olden Cornish times. Do the programme makers take us all for fools? Wake up, aunty Beeb, and grant all of us humble licence holders a bit of intelligence, pleeeeease!

Dawn   Shut up, Mum.

Mother	Oh, look, that car is supposed to have just driven up the drive and it hasn't got a single speck of mud on it. At normal driving speed, you'd be bound to gather some muck, . . . unless they were going at a snail's pace of course. Then it would stay clean.

Pause. She looks baffled. Suddenly stares at the girls.

Mother	A car! In seventeenth-century Cornwall?! Are we all to be taken for fools?
Dawn	Mum, this bit is hundreds of years later.
Mother	Oh. (*Pause.*) And there she is again on horseback, galloping and galloping over the fields . . . (*Pause.*) . . . Galloping and galloping and galloping. That's all they ever do. Gallop. It's physically impossible for *any* horse to gallop for that long. They trot most of the time, anyway, usually. (*Pause.*) If the horse galloped for that long, it'd be dead. This glaring inaccuracy has marred for me an otherwise magnificent evening's viewing.
Jennifer	Mum!
Mother	Oh, adverts. Wind it forward, dear.
Jennifer	No, you can't.
Mother	Don't be sullen. I don't want to watch the adverts, wind it on.
Jennifer	I can't, Mum. The adverts are on the television, aren't they?
Mother	Don't treat me like a fool, you're taping this, aren't you?

Jennifer	Yes, exactly.
Mother	Well then, wind forward please.
Jennifer	I'm taping it, and that's why it's on pause for the adverts, Mum.
Mother	Give me the remote control please so that I can do it myself. (*She presses the buttons.*) Well, now what are we watching? Golf?!
Jennifer	You've changed the channel, Mum.
Dawn	Forget it, I'll watch it later.

They exit. She is left alone, and babbles on.

Mother	Golf! Golf! Golf! Oh dear, oh dear, oh dear. I settled down to enjoy my usual helping of Sunday costume drama with the outstanding young Angarhad Rees, when suddenly, to my dismay, it was cut short and there was golf in its place! They should put a warning on the screen, 'Don't turn over, it's only the golf!' Why, oh why, oh why are we constantly bombarded with endless hours of sport? Do the programme makers really believe this is what we want? When, oh when will auntie Beeb get it right? (*She pushes button.*) I'm sorry, I'm no trickological expert, but even I can tell you that hair conditioner doesn't just work on damaged ends, it doesn't just glow bright red on the bottom of your hair, besides which it is obvious that it is simply a drawing and not a real person. Are we all to be taken for fools? (*She pushes button.*) And P.S., aunty Beeb, I'm very fond of your fine documentaries and your mass exposure of the ever delightful Mr Terry

Wogan and his showbusiness compatriots, but please, oh please could we do something drastic about Selina Scott.

Health Expert

TV AM set – large sofa. Jennifer is the interviewer, Dawn the perennial 'expert'. They never know quite which camera is on.

Jennifer   Welcome back. On the sofa with me today is our resident Health Expert, Dawn French. I'm going to be asking her what's good for our health and what's bad. Dawn, hello.

Dawn   Hello.

Jennifer   So, tell us, Dawn, what is good for our health and what is bad?

Dawn   Things that are generally good for our health are: breathing, walking and reacting to sudden light by blinking.

Jennifer   And what's bad for our health?

Dawn   Bad for our health? Well, heart attacks, comas and gangrene. All of these things are bad for our health.

Jennifer   Can I just say to viewers, we're not trying to make a point here. We're not trying to say anything this morning. That's very interesting, we've been literally flooded with letters asking us what we can and can't eat.

Dawn picks up basket of fruit from side of her.

Dawn   Well, of course, the easy guideline to what we can eat is anything that's edible, for instance Smarties are edible.

Jennifer   Well, that's all very well, but many people are puzzled about what *not* to eat.

Dawn   You'd be surprised at the things that are bad to eat, metal, concrete, wood, don't eat trousers and please, please don't eat instant noodles.

Jennifer   I see, we're surrounded by things we can't eat. Obviously it's very difficult for some of our viewers to make the right decisions with regards to food when faced with *so* much choice. What can they do?

Dawn   My tip is take advice about this from experts. When you're in a food shop, take food from the shelf, hold it up to the assistant and simply ask, 'Excuse me, is this edible?'

Jennifer   Well, I hope that's clarified this murky area and let's all look forward to a happier and healthier life as a result of our little chat here.

Dawn   Do you want to know anything about organic food?

Jennifer   No, that's a bit complicated and political for our viewers. OK, lovely, this is rather nice. (*Touching the food hamper.*)

Dawn   The thing is, a lot of our viewers would simply throw the fruit out of this basket and try to eat the basket.

Jennifer Is it an epidemic?

Dawn Not at the moment.

Fat Aristocrats (Part 1)

*Two large old upperclass women. They are balding
but headscarfed, with hairy old chins. Dressed in
wellington boots or brogues, old jackets and
droopy old dresses. They obviously drive old Land
Rovers and live in run-down country houses
surrounded by labradors. They are tough as nails.*

*Large country kitchen. Run down. A stainless
steel sink piled high with dog bowls and washing
up. The room is full of old horse blankets,
grooming kits, bottles of embrocation. Old hunting
prints on the wall and a couple of old Formica
covered units. Large old table. Old fridge.*

*The two women are sitting at the table having
tea. There is a bottle of whisky standing by the
pot.*

Fat Woman A (Jennifer) Bloody leg.

Hits her leg with a walking stick.

Fat Woman B (Dawn) What's that?

Fat Woman A This bloody leg o' mine, still causing me a bit
of gyp.

Fat Woman B What happened there then?

Fat Woman A   Hit by the bloody Land Rover.

Fat Woman B   Some bloody bastard driving it?

Fat Woman A   No, my bloody Land Rover, forgot to put the handbrake on, came hurtling down the hill, smashed into my bloody leg. Bones and blood everywhere.

Fat Woman B   Out beagling?

Fat Woman A   Yes, a lot of people wanted to see to it you know.

Fat Woman B   A lot of bloody fuss and nonsense.

Fat Woman A   Yes. I don't believe one should give in to these things. Sort themselves out.

Fat Woman B   Leave well bloody alone.

Fat Woman A   I'm not one for a lot of fuss and bother, and nonsense. Look after myself . . .

Fat Woman B   . . . thank you very much.

Fat Woman A   Quite right.

Dawn gets up. Goes to pick up whisky bottle from dresser.

Fat Woman B   Same thing happened to me the other day, out shooting. Some bloody young clot, came up behind me. 12-bore shotgun. Point-blank range. Blast my bloody back open. Everybody saying go to bloody hospital. I said 'Don't be stupid,' lot of fuss and nonsense.

Fat Woman A   Save it for someone who needs it, I say.

Bloody National Health Service, rubbish, lot of mamby pamby nonsense.

Gets up and goes to cut bread on draining board.

Fat Woman B Remember the time I sat on the bloody shooting stick – top came off and the stick went right up me jacksy.

Fat Woman A Nothing wrong with that.

Fat Woman B They all wanted me to get down to the hospital. I said, stop making such a bloody fuss and nonsense. I said let nature take his course. The bloody thing will be out by supper time. And it was!

Fat Woman A lets out a deep yell and puts down the knife. Clutches her hand.

Fat Woman A Damnation, bloody bugger, blood and sand!! Cut me bloody finger off.

Fat Woman B What completely off?

Fat Woman A No, just dangling . . . Oh what the hell, just cut it off completely and be done with it.

Fat Woman B Run it under the cold water tap.

She turns around, hand wrapped in bloodied towel, clutching the amputated finger.

Fat Woman A No, that's a lot of fuss and nonsense. Just cut it off altogether and be done with it. Dogs can have it. (*Throws finger to dogs.*) Here you are, Durbain.

Fat Woman B What about Tibs – she hasn't had one!

Fat Woman A What, one each? OK . . . Come on . . . Come on . . .

Fat Woman A goes back to draining board, cuts fingers off and then throws them to dogs.

Packing

A modern bed-sit. There are various empty suitcases and tote bags around the room. Jackie (Dawn) is in dressing gown and slippers. She has no eyebrows. Knock at door.

Leanne   It's me!

Jackie   Oh, hi Leanne.

Jackie opens door. She has bright orange streaky face and bright orange hands.

Leanne   Hi.

Jackie   Hi, come in. Did you get the tickets?!

Leanne   Yes, I've got them. Don't panic, I went to the travel agent this morning and we've got a special wallet each. It contains luggage tags, itinerary, return ticket and hotel voucher.

Jackie   What about the boarding card!!!!

Leanne   No, I specifically checked that and apparently we are given boarding cards when we check in, which is what we do at the airport. And incidentally, they couldn't tell me exactly which plane we'd be on, they just knew it would be one of their jumbos at this stage.

They sit on bed.

Jackie   Right, I've already had one trial pack and I've tried to be as minimal as possible where clothes are concerned – only four of everything.

Leanne   Have you got your list – skirts, dresses, poncho, halterneck tops, shorts, slacks or jeans? Now, all heavy clothes to wear on the plane for leaving in.

Jackie   Yes, good idea. I'm wearing three pairs of trousers, two shirts, two jumpers, culottes and salopettes.

Leanne   Slippers.

Jackie   Inside the shoes?

Leanne   No, instead of, so you don't get swollen ankles, it is a three-hour flight.

Jackie   I'll take a track suit to change into on board.

Leanne   Underwear – all cotton.

Jackie   All cotton gussets. Vital.

Leanne   Seven bras, one a day, we're not going to want to be washing. And a large bale of paper knickers.

Jackie   Good idea.

Leanne   Shoes, canvas shoes, sling-backs for the evening.

Jackie   Espadrilles, heeled and flat.

Leanne   We might be able to get them out there.

Jackie   No, not in Fuengirola apparently.

Leanne   Boots?

Jackie   Yes, short boots or kinky boots?

Leanne I haven't got any kinky boots, just my patent shoes and wet-look socks.

Jackie Can I take it as read that we're not taking our wellingtons then?

Leanne No. Flip flops. Are you taking a camera?

Jackie Yes, and two cases of film, and a generator.

Leanne Phrasebooks . . .

Jackie Dictionary and thesaurus.

Leanne Paperbacks, cassette player, headphones, mothballs, hangers, washing line, tumble dryer . . .

Jackie And a drying horse. I think we'll only regret it if we don't.

Leanne OK, now toiletries. Make-up remover pads and balls, a large sack of cotton wool, first aid kit including snake vaccine.

Jackie And syringe.

Leanne Yes, foot spray and foot items, earplugs.

Jackie Stop a minute. I had a thought at the office, now what about a telephone directory?

Leanne Ah, no. I've made out a list of important phone numbers. Now suncreams.

Jackie I've got ten different tan factors.

Leanne Calamine lotion?

Jackie No, we must be strict. That's silly.

Leanne Right, contact lenses and fluid?

Jackie	Do you wear contact lenses?
Leanne	No.
Jackie	Well, nor do I. So maybe we don't need the lenses.
Leanne	Right, we'll just take the fluid . . . currency. How many pesetas are you taking?
Jackie	I've got four pesetas changed, no forty pesetas which is ten pounds and fifteen pounds in travellers' cheques.
Leanne	That should be plenty.
Jackie	'Izal', Handy Andy.
Leanne	Twenty rolls soft toilet paper.
Jackie	Yes.
Leanne	Now, things for the beach, two lilos, windbreak, chairs, boiled water, thermos, badminton set, boules, beach bag, swimsuit, swingball and Jakari.
Jackie	Bikini, and full suit.
Leanne	Flippers, snorkel mask. Water-skis?
Jackie	It'll be easier in the long run, rather than hiring in Spanish. Bin bags while I think of them.
Leanne	Crisps, mini kit of everything for the plane. Giant shampoo and giant conditioner, now anything else?
Jackie	Do we need ornaments and a couple of posters for the room?
Leanne	That would be nice but we might be being silly there.
Jackie	Now, let's see your hand luggage arrangement.

Leanne	Right.

Leanne stands up and straps various small bags on to herself, picks up some others.

This is my hand luggage – it's reversible.

She walks around the room demonstrating how she will negotiate the aeroplane.

This is going down the aisle, and this is at check-in. I have a waist band to which I will attach my suitcases to so that I can pull them behind me, all six are on wheels.

Jackie	So, that's your hand luggage.
Leanne	Yes.
Jackie	Very good. My arrangement is much the same but I have a headband over which are counterbalanced my zip-up bag and my back pack.
Leanne	And where will be your passport?
Jackie	Sorry?
Leanne	Where will your passport be?
Jackie	I didn't think I'd need one. Oh no!!
Leanne	Oh no.
Jackie	Do you think I can get one in time? Oh, I am sorry, Leanne. How stupid and silly. I should have checked. Everything had gone far too smoothly, I knew it.
Leanne	Well, I've got a friend that might be able to rush one

through for you. There's a snip of a chance, all may not yet be lost . . .

Jackie   We've only got six months, haven't we?

Leanne   Yes, now, goodness me, is there anything else we've forgotten? Your hair looks nice.

They go towards the kitchen.

Jackie   Yes, Terry did it . . . (*Shouts.*) Take Terry.

Leanne   No. Curling tongs.

Jackie   Oh yes, curling tongs.

Royal Expert

TV AM set – large sofa. Large graphic of Royal crest in the background. Jennifer is the interviewer, Dawn the 'expert'.

Jennifer   Hello, welcome back on the sofa. At the moment we've got our Royal expert with us who I hope is going to give us a little insight into Royal life. Now, Dawn French. Hello and welcome.

Dawn   Hello.

Jennifer   Maybe you would like to tell us, what does the Queen usually have for her mid-morning snack?

Dawn   You're not talking about lunch, are you?

Jennifer   No, her mid-morning snack.

Dawn   And when you say 'usually have', obviously you're not alluding to the toasted slugs or lizards she might have to eat if she was in Riyadh or Tibet around mid-morningish?

Jennifer   No, just the usual mid-morning snack.

Dawn   If she's on the move, going to a large function or an opening or something, I would imagine she probably waits till lunchtime rather than stop off especially for a snack. However, if she's at home, I expect she probably would have a cup of coffee *or* tea, with *or* without milk. She might have a biscuit, perhaps neece or nice biscuits, or bourbons, or gypsy creams or jaffa cakes or hob nob.

Jennifer Oh, so *she* would eat a commoner's biscuit then, not a biscuit specially appointed by the throne?

Dawn No, she likes an ordinary crunch biscuit around mid-morning. Unlike the Queen Mother, of course, who unfortunately because of her teeth situation is reduced to merely sucking when it comes to biscuits.

Jennifer No sandwiches or Danish pastries for the Queen?

Dawn No, not often. Only if she fancies them, she is not forced to eat anything she doesn't like. For instance, she won't usually have anything with a rich sauce around mid-morning, never force-fed.

Jennifer So much like you or I.

Dawn Yes.

Jennifer And the Queen Mum?

Dawn No, just rusks I'm afraid.

Jennifer Now. I think we have time for one last thing. Tell us about napkins.

Dawn Yes, they are usually square and made of cloth or fabric and they either fit in a napkin ring or you can make a design for the plate.

Jennifer Thank you. Lovely. Thank you. Marvellous. Lovely little insight there. Thank you for being with us today.

Dawn   Pleasure. Pleasure. (*Dawn gets up to leave.*)

Jennifer   No, sit there.

They sit waiting for a cue.

Modern Mother and Daughter

Teenager's bedroom. Saffron (Dawn) is sitting at a desk doing homework. There is a knock at the door.

Adriana's voice Darling! Saffy darling, can I come in?

Saffron Mum, I'm working!

Adriana's voice Please, sweetie!

> *Door bursts open and her mother, Adriana, (Jennifer) enters dressed in a huge kaftan.*

Adriana What are you doing, Pushkin, hiding up here all on your own? People will be here soon. What do you think of this? Humphrey bought it for me in Morocco. What do you actually think of it?

> *Saffron is unimpressed.*
> *Adriana takes it off to reveal modern outfit. Acid house gone wrong.*

Adriana No, I knew you wouldn't like it.

Saffron What do you look like?

Adriana I look modern. This is exactly what's happening. I've poured a spritzer for you downstairs, why don't you come down soon? I'm going to ring out for some sushi.

Saffron Ummm, yum, yum.

Adriana Melissa and Jean-Pierre are coming and Bettina's coming over later. She's bringing some of her new jewellery collection that I thought you'd like to see *and* her son Cosimo who you adore.

Saffron I don't adore . . .

Adriana Darling, he's an Adonis. Now stop being such a misery. Come down and have a joint with us later.

Saffron is about to speak.

Adriana Oh all right. Sorry, sorry, sorry I mentioned that. Don't talk about drugs in front of my daughter.

Saffron Well, honestly.

Adriana Honestly what? It doesn't hurt anyone. Some people choose to relax one way, some people . . .

Saffron It turns you into a treacle brain . . .

Adriana Have you read the Warhol diaries I gave you? You must read them. He's so funny, darling. You must read them. (*Pause. Adriana sees a vase on Saffron's shelf.*) Oh, Christ. I completely forgot to ring Janie about those bloody vases for her office. They're stuck in customs in bloody Milan, bloody typical, bugger, bugger, bollocks, bugger – darling, can I take yours, sweetie, I must.

Blows kisses to Saffron.

Saffron You gave that to me for my birthday.

Adriana Thank you, darling. (*Adriana goes and stands nearer to Saffron.*) The car is in the bloody garage. Oh my god *and* my bloody father's dying . . . bore, bore, bore. Sweetie, are you happy? Mmmmm?

Saffron Yes, I'm fine, I've got to get on with this work.

Pause. Adriana sits on the bed and continues to look hard at Saffron.

Adriana Because, I was thinking . . . why don't you want to come with us to Greece this year? It's going to be *so* lovely, Popadopalos is going to lend us his boat, it'll be bliss.

Saffron I really don't want to, Mum.

Very long pause. Adriana looks at Saffron.

Adriana Is it because . . .

Saffron Don't say it, Mum.

Adriana Well . . . is it because?

Saffron I mean it, don't even think about it.

Adriana (*Quickly.*) It's because you don't like being seen in a swimsuit, isn't it, baby? Is it, honey?

Saffron Mum!!!

Adriana Well, it's just I think you'd be a lot happier if you could just shed a few stone, darling.

Saffron No, Mum, *you*'d be a lot happier. Weight shouldn't count, surely it's personality that matters?

Adriana   I'd pay for you, sweetie, to go to that marvellous
man who does Fergie, y'know, with injections. Very
safe, sweetie. Just a couple of little injections,
darling . . . because you've got a beautiful face, and
lovely hair.

Silence. Saffron tries to continue working.

Adriana   Why don't you come with me to Champneys at least
for a week?

Silence. Adriana gets up, trying desperately for attention.

Adriana   (*Sings.*) 'Right on Time, Right on Time.'

Silence.

Adriana   (*Childish anger.*) Is that my Rolex you're wearing?

Saffron   You said I could borrow it.

Adriana   (*Like a child.*) I didn't . . . Give me it back.

Saffron hands back watch.
Silence.

Adriana   (*Starts Buddhist chanting.*) Darling, should I become
a Buddhist? Everyone else says I'd love it. You're so
sensible, you'll know if it's something worth doing.
You just have to chant for things, you know,
holidays and tropical rain forests and things.

Saffron   As long as you don't get involved with any silly
cults.

Adriana   Darling, it's not like crystals, it's not just a fad, it's not like that. Shall I marry Humphrey?

Saffron   He's gay.

Adriana   We adore each other, he's asked me, and we'd get this house.

Saffron   What about Jean-Pierre, I thought he was your boyfriend?

Adriana   Well, he hasn't got a house, has he? I'm fed up with always living in other people's houses, aren't you?

Saffron   I can't keep up with all your boyfriends.

Adriana   And Jean-Pierre is *ma chérie maintenant, seulement.* (*Pause. Adriana drops dramatically to the floor.*) Ow, my back's killing me. I had a Shiatsu this morning. Darling, you wouldn't . . . (*Indicates she wants Saffron to massage her.*)

Saffron   No, I won't rub your back. I'm really sorry, Mum, but I've got to get this homework done by the morning.

Adriana   (*Gets up quickly in a huff.*) Don't call me 'Mum'.

Saffron   Sorry . . . Mummy, Mummy, Mummy.

Adriana   Stop it! You're far too old to be calling me that. Call me Adriana.

She wanders round the room.

We must get a help. Veronica says to get a Filipino, they work like buggers and cost flap-all. (*Icy glare from Saffron.*) Oh, don't look at me like that. Look at you looking at me with your father's eyes. You can be a socialist and have staff . . . darling. (*Picks up photo from Saffron's desk.*) Have you seen the bastard recently?

Saffron   Are you referring to Dad?

Adriana   Oh, don't justify his puny little existence by giving him a title, please.

Saffron   Yes, I saw him yesterday.

Adriana flips her lid.

Adriana   I don't know why you don't just go and live with the bloody prick full time, you seem to bloody love him so much! Honestly, you don't consider my feelings at all! Nobody ever does! Well, bollocks to all of you. (*Throws herself dramatically on bed.*)

Saffron   (*Unmoved.*) Stop swearing, Mum, it's not clever, it's not funny and no one's the slightest bit impressed.

Adriana   (*Pause.*) Oh, sweetie. I'm sorry. (*Pause.*) Adriana needs a cuddle . . . darling.

Saffron   Hard luck.

Adriana   You old bitch. (*Pause.*) Look all I'm trying to do is talk to you . . . All right, all right. Can I talk to you, pushkin? Come here.

Saffron gets up and goes reluctantly to sit next to her mother on the bed.

Saffron   Don't touch me.

Adriana   It's about university, darling, do you have to go?

Saffron   Yes I do.

Adriana   Do you have to do physics? I mean, can't you do one arts subject for god's sake, then you could do some work for me, darling. I mean, what am I supposed to do at parties, say, 'Here's my daughter, the bloody old scientist,' and talk about test tubes and chemicals? I don't want a daughter who's a fat, old, dowdy spinster. Nobody will want you.

Saffron   Have you quite finished?

Adriana   No. Where is it you're going?

Saffron   Aberdeen.

Adriana   Aberdeen! Aberbloodydeen, I won't be able to cope with you in Aberbloodydeen. You're the only one who knows where anything is here. I can't even find the coffee on my own, darling. It's just all too awful. Oh god, I just don't know if I'll ever be able to cope. (*Gets up and walks to desk.*)

Saffron   Mum, calm down. You're getting yourself in such a state. You've got a lot of good friends here. Look, if you really can't cope, after three months I'll come back and look after you.

Adriana   (*Victorious.*) Thank you, sweetie. Now, you will come down later, won't you? (*Goes to leave.*) But if you come down and there's food out, please don't eat anything. I've told everyone you're on a diet.

Saffron   Mum, Mum, can you turn that music down a bit. (*Reaches for condoms.*) Oh, and Mum, I checked your bedside table and I noticed you'd run out of these. (*Holds up packet of condoms.*) Is Jean-Pierre staying tonight? Take these (*hands over condoms*) and please use them.

Adriana blows her a kiss and heads out, dancing.

Record Choice

Desert Island Discs *type programme, about to go on air. The host/interviewer, well-dressed, middle-aged woman (Jennifer) waits impatiently for her guest (Dawn).*

Jennifer (*Whispering.*) Why isn't she here? Where is she?

Dawn comes in.

Dawn Sorry, sorry.

Jennifer Oh, you got here. Was the traffic bad? Was it?

Dawn Sorry I'm late, nice to meet you.

Jennifer We're going live in a few moments but . . .

Dawn OK.

Jennifer Could you just possibly just spare a moment, just speak into that and give us a level.

Dawn Err yes, hello, err I'm here today, it's taken me a long time in the traffic. (*Laughs nervously.*)

Jennifer Right, we're about to go.

Dawn OK.

Pause. Jennifer gets a signal they are on the air.

Jennifer   (*In a deep mellow voice.*) My guest today on *Record Choice* is best known for her work amongst the poor, destitute and wounded in war-torn Beirut. She is an expert on childhood diseases and a well-respected figure in the medical field. Together with all this she still finds time to be a devoted mother of two. She was last year's Woman of the Year. She is Dr Eleanor Wood. Dr Eleanor. Welcome.

Dawn   Thank you.

Jennifer   Before we go for your Record Choice, let's see if we can paint a picture of the young Eleanor Wood, and maybe recall a few childhood memories for you. You excelled in school academically and at sport. I love to imagine the picture of you, this Cornish dumpling, probably goalie in the hockey team, cheerfully bouncing around in goal, lifting everyone's spirits. You were, I should imagine, a happy, jolly, sturdy person.

Dawn   I suppose so.

Jennifer   (*Not letting her get a word in.*) The class clown perhaps? So many people with physical disadvantages like yourself often end up compensating. Was it, dare I say, your chunkiness, the fact that you were and are a fuller-figured person, that made you more determined to succeed?

Points at Dr Eleanor without looking up from notes.

Dawn   I hadn't thought about it. Perhaps.

Jennifer	Perhaps being a bulkier figure you may not have had boyfriends, probably not, and therefore more time to study. But we don't need to dwell here. You are married now to Derek Wood. Well done! Is he a tubby or a normal person?
Dawn	I'm sorry, what did you say?
Jennifer	Well, I just rather like the image of two plumps finding consolation, even a bit of pleasure, who knows, in each other's arms. You have succeeded where other tubby people have failed.
Dawn	No. This bears no relevance . . .
Jennifer	But we don't want to dwell there. We want to talk about the real you. Because you are one of our larger ladies, you're obviously not ashamed of your rotund, rather lovely bounciness, your ampleness, your huggable, bosomy chestiness.
Dawn	Why don't you just say 'fat'?
Jennifer	Pardon?
Dawn	Why don't you just say, 'Welcome, Fattie!', and then it'll all be over and done with?
Jennifer	You're running yourself down there. 'Hello, Chunky' is as far as we could go.
Dawn	Oh all right, you can describe me as chunky, ample, bubbly, huggable and so on, so long as I can describe you as slow-witted, uninteresting, obtuse, *dull*, tedious, mentally stagnant . . . Because what you're really wanting to say about me is 'fat' and what I'm skirting round about you is 'stupid'.

Pause.

Jennifer   I think I'm having my leg pulled here. We're not here to talk about me.

Dawn   No, we're not, so ask me a question about work.

Jennifer   All right, a question about work – here we go. (*Begins again.*) I'm here with Dr Eleanor Wood. Now Dr Eleanor, to get serious for a moment. In war-torn Beirut, there's obviously a lot of suffering and hardship (*Pause.*) Food shortages? Perhaps you could tell us how a person like you might cope with that sort of situation, being the sort of person you obviously are.

Dawn   What sort of person is that?

Jennifer   A (*long pause*) piggy.

Dawn   (*Gets up.*) I'm sorry. That's it.

Jennifer   I'm sorry. Please stay, we'll cut that.

Dawn   Well, honestly.

Jennifer   We'll move on. I wonder if I can ask you, Dr Eleanor, quickly before you go. One luxury in life you could not imagine living without. This is normally a light-hearted moment. Could you say something like a fridge full of Mars Bars? But anything goes.

Dawn   Right now I'd like a Sten-gun.

Jennifer   I think that would probably be a chocolate Sten-gun.
    And that just about concludes the programme today. I've been squidged into the studio with the

large personality that is Dr Eleanor Wood, but before we hear her Record Choice, time for me just to say I'll be back next week with a more slimline *Record Choice* when our guest will be the lovely talented (and thankfully) *petite* Jane Asher. Here now is Dr Wood's Choice.

Music plays 'Hey, Fattie Boom Boom'.

Extras

It is the foot of the cross in Martin Scorsese's Last
Temptation. *Mary Magdalen and two peasants are
there next to our extras. They are all looking up at
Jesus. We see his feet at the top of the frame. All are
weeping.*
Director through loud hailer shouts, 'Cut!'

Jean   I think we've cut.

Dorothy   Oh good, d'you fancy a sherry? I've got a flask-full
in my props basket.

Jean   He's very good isn't he?

Dorothy   (*Looking up at Christ.*) Oh yes.

Jean   No, not him. I mean the director.

Dorothy   Oh, Mr Scorsese?

Jean   Yes. What else has he done?

Dorothy   Um. *Taxi* . . . I think.

Jean   Oh, the sit-com with Danny De Vito?

Dorothy   Yes, and that film with Jodie Foster, where she's an
under-age prostitute.

Jean   *The Brady Bunch?*

Dorothy   That's it, yes.

Jean   But he's good too. (*Indicates actor on cross.*) Chuck, or whatever he's called. I never imagined Jesus as American somehow, always firmly believed he was English.

Dorothy   Yes. But my favourite will always be Robert Powell. Now, he really looked like our Lord, didn't he?

Jean   Yes, and Charlton Mason was a lovely Moses.

Dorothy   D'you know, I could listen to that man's voice all day . . . it's just like liquid silk. They always give him a beard, don't they?
(*Pointing up at cross.*)

Jean   I expect it was harder to shave in Jewish times.

Dorothy   It also deflects the sun, you see.

Jean   Yes. (*Goes dreamy.*) It must have been lovely in those days.

Dorothy   Just sitting all day on the beach, watching the fishermen. Those 'fishers of men'.

Jean   And talking about God.

Dorothy   And having many multitudes of women to wash your feet with Gold, Frankenstein and Myrrh.

Jean   Yes, Myrrh.

Dorothy   Funny word, isn't it? – Myrrh. Say it quickly, Myrrh, Myrrh. (*Jean joins in.*) Sounds like 'murmur', doesn't it? Of course, Scottish people say 'myrrrrrh'.

Actor on cross says 'SHHH.'

Jean   (*Looks up.*) Oooh, the look he gave you then.

Dorothy   Are we about to go again? Because I've got some ideas in my props basket. I'm going to be a person who's hard of sight. (*She brings out sunglasses and fold-away white stick.*)

Jean   Oh that's good, and I could be your guide. Because you *would* have one, wouldn't you?

Dorothy   Yes. I'd be up here hoping for one last miracle, wouldn't I?

Jean   Yes. How's your costume after this morning?

Dorothy   D'you know, this skirt is only just dry now.

Jean   It was worth it though, Dorothy, honestly, it looked spectacular when you threw yourself off that high rock into the River Jordan in the baptism scene.

Dorothy   I was being a desperate leper, you see.

Jean   Oh yes. Lucky John the Baptist was there to break your fall, otherwise it would have been a terrible belly flop. It's strange that they used a river for that scene, because usually you get baptised in a pont in church.

Dorothy   Yes. A what, sorry?

Jean   A pont.

Dorothy   No, no, no. Do you mean near the culprit where the vicar stands? That's the punt. It's called the *punt*.

Jean   Oh.

They both laugh.

Dorothy Do you know the difference between the Catholic and the Anglican Church?

Jean No.

Dorothy Oh well, the Anglicans don't like Madonna.

Jean Madonna?

Dorothy Not *the* Madonna . . . as in Mrs Sean Penn.

Jean Oh, not the Madonna . . . I should be a virgin . . . (*She sings like Kylie Minogue's* 'I Should Be So Lucky'.)

Dorothy No, a Madonna, the Mother of Our Lord. Anglicans won't be having her . . . just our friend here. (*Indicates Christ.*)

Director shouts 'Stand-by.'

Jean Oh, I think they're ready.

Dorothy Oh good . . . (*Puts on sunglasses.*) Do you think it would be a good idea to raise our voices to the Lord during this take?

Jean Yes, why not? We *would*, wouldn't we? (*She sings. Director shouts 'Action.'*) Day by day, day by day . . .'

Dorothy joins in.

Dorothy 'Jesus Christ, Superstore . . .'

Director shouts 'Cut.'

Jean   (*As if listening to him.*) Sorry?

Dorothy   Something wrong?

Hollywood Expert

TV AM set – large sofa. Jennifer is the interviewer, Dawn the 'expert'.

Jennifer   Welcome back. With us on the sofa we've got our Hollywood expert, Dawn French, and she's going to be giving us a little peek into the life of one of our favourite stars – the lovely Joan Collins. So Dawn, what would a day in the life of, say, Joan Collins be like?

Dawn   Well, she'd usually be kissed awake by George Hamilton III or someone like that, she'd open her eyes dreamily and immediately see herself in the huge mirror above her enormous heart-shaped bed with the red satin sheets and furry bearskin bed cover. She would step out of bed in her silky matching nightie and housecoat and might step into, say, a couple of pink mules.

Jennifer   I think we've got a picture of some mules haven't we?

Shows picture of mules.

Dawn   Yes, that's right, that sort of thing, and she'd go to the bathroom where a maid should have already drawn her bath with masses of bubbles or

sometimes just mink oil and candles all around it
and champagne in a big ice bucket on the side. I
expect Kris Kristofferson would probably pop over
to slip in beside her and rub her back with a huge
loofah. She would usually learn her lines in the bath
whilst sipping champagne and she'd take phone
calls on a marble telephone from Aaron Spelling
and Michael Caine and Anthony Newley, that sort
of person. And then she'd be rubbed down with
gigantic pink towels.

Jennifer Oh yes, we've got a picture of towels.

Shows picture of towels.

Dawn Yes, that's right, exactly like that. She'd float to her
wardrobe and select a fur coat and perhaps some
Janet Reger silky undies, she doesn't usually need
to wear anything else, and she'd walk out to a huge
white stretch limo, and she'd usually chuck credit
cards at the servants.

Jennifer Ordinary credit cards?

Dawn Oh no, emerald and diamond encrusted ones so
they can do the shopping for supper. Then she
usually climbs into the limo and opens the drinks
cabinet while a swarthy chauffeur looks at her in the
rear-view mirror suspiciously because he's a
terrorist who usually then takes her, this is around
10 a.m., to a remote airstrip where she's flown to a
small obscure kingdom like, say, Latvania, where
she has to go to prison and get mud on her
shoulder and wait for Dex to come and boldly
rescue her.

'She'd be kissed awake by George Hamilton III.'

Miss Saunders as Miss Day, wishing she had
a man and a dress with sleeves.

'Miss French as Miss Taylor. It's amazing what
a good corset and an eyebrow pencil can do.'

A couple
of mean
old bags.

'It's reversible, Jackie.'

The lights and glamour are all
too much for Dawn as they relax
on set during the shooting of
their Christmas movie.

Relaxing on set. A wonderful moment captured.

Our hommage to
the lovely Julia
Andrews and the
old nun.

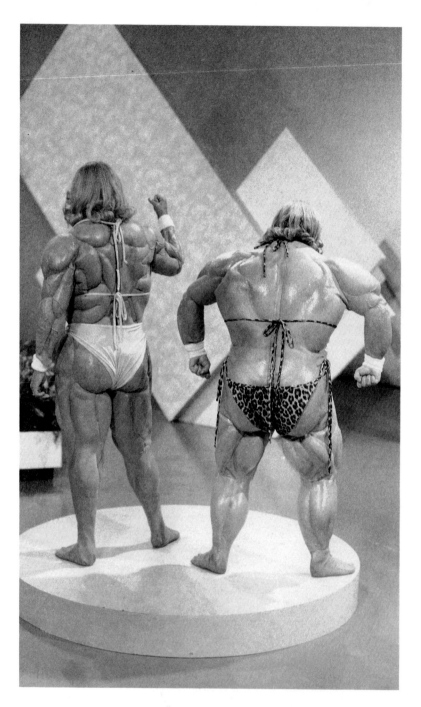

Keeping in shape
has never been a problem for us.

The lovely Mavis Nicholson
looking rather jealous.

At home. Dawn
contemplating life on a
desert island with Oliver
Reed.

Jennifer gets to stuff her
face. Any excuse!

Our hommage to opera.
We are joined by the
lovely Sarah Walker and
the lovely Carl Davis.

Pause.

Dawn   She's usually back in time for a première in the evening though.

Jennifer   I see, well thank you very much. Lovely little insight there.

Dawn   Do you want to know about Britt Ekland?

Jennifer   No.

Dawn   Nobody wants to know about Britt Ekland.

Woman's World

*Inside the office of the two editors of a women's magazine.
There are two desks. There are hundreds of back issue
front covers, with only Princess Di or Jean Boht on the
cover. The office is crammed with 'womanly' trivia,
catalogues, freebies, Marks and Spencer food, cups and
saucers, pretty ruched curtains, chairs covered in Liberty
fabrics and a huge pin-board on which there is a layout of
the plans for the upcoming edition of the magazine.
Fiona (Dawn) is busily pinning up more layouts. She is a
well co-ordinated vision in bright silks and large red
glasses.
Enter Gill (Jennifer) with lots of carrier bags, huge
handbag and briefcase. She is a prime example of a mail
order victim.*

Gill   Morning, I've been thinking about it *all* night, Fiona,
and I think I've got it . . . Since it's the bumper Easter
issue . . . bonnets.

Fiona   Bliss . . . of course . . . bonnets.

Gill   We'll get lots of back issues with pictures of Di in
various hats. Isn't it wild and perfect?
Now what have we got? Any news from Tim Dalton?

Fiona   Yes, his people have come back. He'll do it so long as
he can talk about the new Bond.

Gill	Right, well I think we put him in an Arran and wellies and do 'At home with Bond'.
Fiona	Yes, yes. Not at his home, I hope.
Gill	No, mine, in front of my French windows. Like we did with Anthony Andrews.
Fiona	And we'll call it. . . ?
Gill	Bond, Bond . . . Beautiful Bond? No . . . Terrific Tim? No . . . Tiny Tim? No. Tim Talks?
Fiona	Bond . . . Bond Voyage? No. Premium Bond?
Gill	Perfect, perfect, perfect.
Fiona	I'll get back to Nigel Havers' people and say no.
Gill	Tell them he *could* do a recipe this week, but next week we could do a 'Nigel really is terrific' piece. (*Shouting off.*) Sue, say no to Nigel Havers this week – we're going with Timmy Dalton.
Fiona	I'll write a few letters for postbag this week saying how fab Tim Dalton is and a couple of 'When are we going to see more of Nigel Havers?' . . . or something like that?
Gill	Perfect. Ah yes, now, meant to talk to you about problem page, Fiona, not enough emotion.
Fiona	Well I've written to us with three emotional letters this week.
Gill	Yes?
Fiona	First one is 'Fancy my best friend's husband, what should I do?'
Gill	'Think he feels the same way', that sort of thing?

Fiona	Yes. And the second one is 'Think my best friend's husband has left her but I'm too embarrassed to ask'.
Gill	The answer being a sort of 'She'll tell you in her own time' type of thing?
Fiona	Yes. The third one is 'Not interested in sex anymore – am I abnormal?'
Gill	No, say 'Perfectly normal. If worried, see doctor, he'll give you some pills.' Don't forget to do a 'My daughter's on heavy drugs' item and a letter on Aids: 'Is it all stuff and nonsense?'
Fiona	I'd have to mention sex.
Gill	Oh, then no, drop it, drop it. Now, cover.
Fiona	Well we've got a choice this week, Gilly. Princess Di or Jean Boht.

Holds up picture of both.

Gill	No competition.
Fiona	Jean Boht?
Gill	Absolutely.
Fiona	We could have her with that pottery chicken from *Bread*, take the top off, and fill it with lots of little Easter chicks inside – what do you think?
Gill	'Jean's EASTER JOY!' Marvellous. I don't want to see any primary colours on that cover, only pastels. Gwen, Gwen, something on conservatories. Ask Hannah Gordon or the lovely Susan Hampshire.
Fiona	I thought Shakira Caine on multi-purpose sarongs.

Gill   Good idea.

Fiona   Wait a minute, Gill – sarongs are a *bit* like saris – so we get Shakira on sarongs leading nicely into saris leading nicely into Benazir Bhutto.

Gill   That's our serious piece.

Fiona   We then have the option of putting Benazir's head on Margaret Thatcher's body and vice versa and that would show our readers what two leading women would look like in each other's clothes.

Both   That's our politics.

Gill   Perfect, absolutely perfect. Now, ads? Are we carrying tampons this week?

Fiona   (*Very blatant.*) I thought we'd have pantie pads.

Gill   Yes. I mean there's only one place a tampon's going.

Fiona   That reminds me, Sue Lawley on flans?

Gill   No. Too spiky.

Phone rings. Fiona answers.

Fiona   Hello, oh. (*To Gill.*) It's Janey again.

Gill   Asher or Seymour?

Fiona   Asher.

Gill   What does she want?

Fiona   Wants us to cover her kitchen again.

Gill   Oh no. Is there a new angle?

Fiona   (*Into phone.*) Is there a new angle in the kitchen? Done this so many times. Yes? Oh, hand-painted Mexican tiles.

They both pull a face.

Gill   No, not Mexican. Say no, but offer her the flan feature.

Fiona   Have to pass on the tiles, bit too ethnic for us – but what about 'It's flantastic' – something about you and flans? Yes? Great. Bye. She's gone for it, novelty flans.

Gill   Might clash with kids' kitchen.

Fiona   Sue! Can I see the layout for kids' kitchen, pleeeese!

Gill   And Sue! If you're on your feet you couldn't pop down to Marksy's for our lunch, could you? Thank you.

Fiona   Now, Mandy Smith for anything?

Gill   No.

Fiona   Kate Adie?

Gill   What, for a make-over?

Fiona   No. I know she needs a make-over but I've promised it to Sarah's daughter this week.

Gill   Oh well, maybe a travel feature – romantic hot-spots. I know, in Beirut. I've also been thinking Barbara Bush! She's marvellous, isn't she? 'Bumptious, Big, Beautiful, Ballsy Barbara goes grey gracefully . . .' something like that? Fiona? . . . What's the matter?

Fiona has a sudden turn and is wandering around as if in a dream.

Fiona It's happening to me again, Gill, I'm sorry. It's suddenly dawned on me that this whole thing is so trivial . . .

Gill Come on, darling, don't be like that . . . Come on now . . . Pull through . . .

Fiona . . . so pointless . . . it doesn't mean anything . . .

Gill Come on, sweetie . . . pull through, pull through. We haven't discussed horoscopes yet, come on, pull through, or knitwear . . . come on . . . you can do it . . .

Fiona Yes, I *do* like horoscopes . . . and there's always the Bride of the Year competition . . . that's important. It's someone's most important day. Isn't it?

Gill Of course it is, darling. Now, story. What have we got?

Fiona A thriller by Fay Weldon, seven hundred words, called *He Took Me* . . .

Gill Too racy! Cut it in half and call it *Regrets* . . .

Fiona Right.

Gill So, join me on the sofa for a sum-up meeting . . . We've got Jean's Joy as a cover, and everything I've already mentioned – Di's Easter bonnets, Tim Dalton at home. I know I say it every week, but can't we get Charles Dance to do something?

Fiona Sue! Charles Dance to do anything.

Gill (*Reading list.*) Hodge Podge. What's that?

Fiona Patricia Hodge, back in shape after her baby.

Gill Lovely. Now, jumpers. Knits are under control, aren't they? (*Shouts.*) Miranda! Now politics.

Fiona Yes. Bhutto and Babs Bush and Lulu.

Gill Lovely. Now, science?

Fiona Well, we've got 'Flossing can be fun'.

Gill Right, OK. Triumph over tragedy story? I don't see anyone.

Fiona Sarah Greene.

Gill Oh yes, all right, that's lovely, and get her to do a salad as well. That will cover environmental issues.

Fiona Of course, 'Greene's Green Greens'.

Gill Now, coping with surgery?

Fiona Yes, Miriam's turned up trumps again. 'Stars and their secret scars'.

Gill Oh, that's marvellous. Horoscopes, competition, and a free J-cloth offer. That's the bulk of it.

Fiona We can pad with items from old back issues . . .

Gill As per normal. I think that's lunch, Fiona, and a quick afternoon flick through Freeman's.

She picks up mail order catalogue.

Gill (*Shouting off.*) Chicken tikka sandwiches, Sue, and a three-bean salad for me.

Fiona Oh, go crazy, Sue – two syrup sponges.

Both start flicking through catalogues.

Fat Aristocrats (Part 2)

They enter the kitchen. They are dressed slightly smarter – dresses, husky waistcoats, and headscarves, wellington boots. They are carrying Sporting Life, *binocular cases with racing tags all over them, and handbags. Very red in the cheeks.*

Fat Woman A   (Jennifer) Bloody good day!

Fat Woman B   (Dawn) Bloody marvellous day.

Both sit.

Fat Woman A   Do you want some tea?

Fat Woman B   Right o'.

Fat Woman A produces a bottle of whisky from her binocular case and pours some into two old teacups.

Fat Woman A   There we go. Picked it up at the wedding.

Fat Woman B   What a bloody dull do. Bride looked a fright, I thought.

Fat Woman A   What a fright! Like some old bitch on heat, I thought. Pig in dress. She may be my daughter but I'll have to agree with you there!

Fat Woman B Thank god we had a reason to get away.

Fat Woman A Yes, well I always told her we had to be at Haydock for the 2.30 so not to arrange it around us, but there you are.

Fat Woman B Ugly bugger she's married. Ugly bugger. Is he a foreigner?

Fat Woman A Welsh, you know, Welsh.

Fat Woman B How could she?

Fat Woman A Even worse, a doctor, a doctor.

Fat Woman B Not a stupid bloody bugger doctor?

Fat Woman A He's the stupid ass that tried to call an ambulance for me that time.

Fat Woman B What?

Fat Woman A You remember that time I felt a bit dizzy and lost the feeling down one side. Do you remember that?

Fat Woman B Unconscious, weren't you?

Fat Woman A Just for a couple of days, nothing much. Just a minor coronary. Lot of fuss and bloody nonsense about it.

Fat Woman B Fuss and nonsense. Something happened to me. Do you remember the time when I fell down the cellar stairs, cellar stairs do you remember, cracked my head open, lay unconscious with gangrene for three weeks, down there. Until some nosy bugger from the village . . .

Fat Woman A Neighbourhood witch, was it?

Fat Woman B Yes. Noticed I wasn't bringing in my milk, looked through the post box and saw the dogs crapping all over the house, so he decided to alert the constabulary . . .

Fat Woman A Fuss and nonsense.

Fat Woman B Who came and broke the bloody door down.

Fat Woman A Unnecessary bloody to-do. Nosy parkers, can't bear them.

Fat Woman B I only escaped going to the hospital then because they thought I was dead.

Fat Woman A Bloody lucky, by jingo, by the sound of it! Bloody lucky, I mean lot of fuss and nonsense there was when George passed away. Do you remember?

Fat Woman B What?

Fat Woman A The other week when George passed away.

Fat Woman B George.

Fat Woman A Husband. You know George. Stupid looking bugger, gammy leg.

Fat Woman B Oh yes. George.

Fat Woman A (*Gets rather maudlin.*) Very sick at the end, poor George. Very sick.

Fat Woman B Bad luck.

Fat Woman A Stripped of his faculties. Took me aside, asked me if I'd help speed up the going . . . put him out of his misery with a bit of dignity.

Fat Woman B And did you, dear?

Fat Woman A Had to. Hit him over the head with a shovel and dumped him on the bonfire.

Fat Woman B Well, it's what he would have wanted. Marvellous compost.

Fat Woman A Yes, absolutely.

Fat Woman B Why not.

Fat Woman A Anyway, hoping the daughter's not going to breed.

Fat Woman B Oh god.

Fat Woman A Don't want a whole lot of Welsh sprogs coming round.

Fat Woman B Get the dogs to eat 'em.

Fat Woman A Cheers!

Elizabethans

Two Elizabethan hags in an alehouse. They are both filthy and covered in pox – the typical housewives of their day. (Put on a West Country accent and blacken your teeth for best effect.)

Dawn So, Mistress Beth. How's your son, not your youngest one, not the poxie one that died last week?

Jennifer Oh, George.

Dawn The giant!

Jennifer (*Laughing.*) Yes, giant's the word, he's not stopped growing you know.

Dawn Really!

Jennifer He's four foot two now, he can barely get in the front door. Towers above me. Well, he's an actress.

Dawn Oh.

Jennifer Yes, with Shakespeare's Company.

Dawn Really, what's he up to at the moment then?

Jennifer Well, they're rehearsing this new play at the moment called *MacBeth*. He's playing the Good Fairy.

Dawn Comedy then.

Jennifer   Comedy, yes, not working though. They've got a bank of writers on it but he's still having to come home at night and work on the script himself, you know. Trying to get lines to rhyme, that sort of thing.

Dawn   Would I have seen him in anything?

Jennifer   The last thing he did was *Romeo and Juliet*. Did you see that? He was Juliet.

Dawn   Did they tape up his Adam's apple?

Jennifer   Oh, that wasn't all they taped up.

Much bawdy laughter.

Dawn   Oh, I have seen him, he was good the night I went, but the audience reaction was poor, though.

Jennifer   Quiet?

Dawn   Yes, no bawdy laughter, no one prancing on stage trying to squeeze his pomanders, no one throwing any old vegetables at him, or pissing all over him or anything like that. So boring.

Jennifer   Well, everyone's at home worrying about the pox. That's the problem.

Dawn   You see, I don't hold with this modern theatre business. There was barely a toga to be seen when I saw *Antony and Cleopatra* the other day. I wrote to Shakespeare and told him about it. I said, 'Mr Shakespeare, an otherwise magnificent evening's entertainment was marred for me by the offensive size of some codpieces on the stage.'

Jennifer Yes. Did you see my son at the Globe?

Dawn Yes, lovely the Globe, isn't it?

Jennifer I wonder how the Rose Theatre is getting on?

Dawn looks at Jennifer in astonishment.

Dawn Mistress Beth! You really do not listen to the town crier at all, do you?

Jennifer What, have I missed something?

Dawn They never built the Rose Theatre.

Jennifer Oh no! (*Realises her error. Cackles.*)

Dawn No, they built some foundations and so on and builders stood around eating a lot of hazelnuts contemplating the whole thing, then they ran out of money.

Jennifer Oh that's right.

Dawn Apparently, Shakespeare's putting a codpiece factory on that site now.

Jennifer Oh really. (*Laughs.*) Doesn't miss a trick, he's a canny old beardy baldy pate. (*Pause.*) It's funny that women don't wear codpieces, isn't it? Funny that.

Dawn looks amazed.

Dawn What are you talking about? What would we put in them?

Jennifer You could put your satsumas in there.

Both laugh.

Dawn   You know, I think you're two farthings short of a
             sixpence, you are. You ought to go and see the
             apothecary, get some leeches and hornets. Sort
             yourself out. Or you could come home with me and
             my Phillip will give you a good sucking.

Jennifer (*Surprised and laughing.*) Oh yes, I've heard that one
             before.

Dawn   With . . . his . . . new . . . leeches of course.

             Both cackle. Jennifer notices a wench playing up to a
             man in the corner.

Jennifer Oh . . . yes . . . Look at that over there (*Shouts.*)
             Whore!

Dawn   That's my daughter.

Jennifer Oh, sorry. (*Jennifer shouts again.*) Trollop!!

Dawn   Thanks.

             Both cackle.

Space Expert

*TV AM set. Jennifer on set. Obviously nothing to say.
Doesn't know what's next.*

Jennifer   Welcome back. And our guest has left us and I'm
on the sofa with our expert, Dawn French. So what
are you being an expert about today? What have you
got that we can talk about this morning?

Dawn   Er. Well, have there been any disasters, 'plane
crashes?

Jennifer   No, I'm afraid not. (*Looks around studio for help.*)

Pause.

Dawn   Romania.

Jennifer   Don't touch Romania.

Dawn   Facial hair.

Jennifer   No, Clare's got that.

Dawn   Any pregnant Royals been skiing?

Jennifer   (*Listening to ear-piece.*) Well now I think we'll go for
our poetry spot. Now here's a lovely poem sent in
by Mrs Riley. (*Looking at it.*) It's called 'Our
Wedding Day' – it's a rather touching poem.

Clears throat.

   'A Wedding Day'

   Through the gloom and troubles
   That is always on the news they say
   Comes a ray of hope and sunshine
   My daughter Lesley's wedding day.

Smiles soppily.

   She who was once a toddler grew
   Played, had colds, and birthdays
   And I changed her nappies. Phew!

Well it seems to end there and that's rather lovely.
Well, thank you, Mrs Riley.

Dawn	Just been thinking. I'm an Expert on space.
Jennifer	Right. Well. The Americans are putting a lot of space-shuttles up into space at the moment. What must it be like to be in space?
Dawn	Well, I was actually thinking about hanging space. Anyway, what must it be like to be in space? I think it must be lonely.
Jennifer	Really. Do you need training?
Dawn	Training is very necessary.
Jennifer	(*Getting serious.*) Let's cut through this. People shouldn't imagine it's the sort of thing they can just do.
Dawn	No, in fact I'll prepare a fact sheet for anyone interested.

Jennifer   Lovely. So if you're thinking of going into space send in for a fact sheet. Thank you.

Dawn   Thank you.

Publishing

Groucho Club: dining room. Lunchtime. Judith (Jennifer) is sitting alone at a table for two. She is flicking through some new paperbacks and literary magazines. She is in her late thirties – and works for a publishing firm. Jo approaches the table. She is a writer, slightly more relaxed than Judith. Judith stands to greet her.

Judith   Jo, hello.

Jo   Hello, Judith.

They both sit.

Judith   Drink?

Jo   Why not?

Judith   I've ordered some wine, so shall we talk first and then order, then we can enjoy the food after the business.

Jo   Fine, fire away.

Judith   Firstly and foremostly, I'd like to say vis-à-vis the last meeting that we are delighted that you have chosen to come with us, and to say that we really intend to give this book our very best shot.

Jo   Good.

Judith   I've prepared the background information on us you
asked for, and some projected information and
figures for the forthcoming year.

Passes over some sheets of paper.

You'll see on Sheet Three a list of other authors and
projected sales predictions.

Jo   These are people who are writing books?

Judith   Who have shown an interest in books.

Jo   You have signed them?

Judith   Virtually . . . well, we've rung them up. What you're
looking at is a future projection of potential sales of
potential authors should they decide to sign with us.

Jo turns the page.

Jo   The figures are very impressive.

Judith   Aren't they? They should give you an overall picture
of projects past and present.

Jo   There's a number here, what's that –? Next to this list
– a number 10.

Judith   Ignore that.

Jo   What is it?

Judith   It's not relevant, you needn't concern . . .

Jo   I'm interested.

Judith   (*Quickly.*) It's just the number of people in the office.

Jo   And down here . . .

Judith   Look, don't pay any attention to the figures – they are just projections.

Jo   What are these figures?

Judith   That is a rough estimate of the kind of figure we're thinking of.

Jo   For?

Judith   The overall projection . . . of . . . Autumn. Look, Jo, if I can for a moment just speak from the hip, ignore the figures.

Jo   Oh right. (*Puts down the paper.*)

Judith   Onwards from there, I would just like to say vis-à-vis the buzz in the office – I have to say that since we learned that you were on board the buzz has been tremendous. We are rearing to go but keen not to put any pressure on you at this moment. Juliette and Samantha are ready to help you with anything you need – and are very keen.

Jo   What do Juliette and Samantha actually do? I'm writing and illustrating the book, so what's their job?

Judith   Really just there to pester you with phone calls.

Jo   That's why I haven't been able to write really, they keep phoning me all the time. You see, I don't need them for anything at the moment.

Judith   You don't need them for anything at the moment . . . No, all right, but you must let them pester you just a bit . . . I'll arrange a lunch so you can meet them, and put names to voices and faces to noses.

Jo   About the lunches?

Judith   Yes, this is just the first of many, let me assure you.

Jo   Good. It was just that you hadn't mentioned them until now. Also, I want you to know that with this book, I'm changing direction, Judith, the style is different, the whole feeling is *much* more . . . free and I really do want to feel that I've got your full support for that, and entire artistic freedom.

Judith   Can I stop you there, Jo. Do you want to cover it all on this lunch?

Jo   Yes. I think so. I'm considering hardback, Judith, I don't mind telling you.

Judith   Ah, well, yes, everything is possible Jo . . . I just want to run past you the thoughts we've had in the office regarding size – I've brought this mock-up (*Produces four-inch square piece of card.*) It's called the stocking-filler size.

Jo   Yes, that's about the size, but not as thick I hope?

Judith   No. But this actual size *sells*, you see, we were thrilled with *Mr Man's Willy* last Christmas, it literally leapt off the shelves . . . so we can take it that this would be the optimum size for *Rock Stars and Their Toilet Seats*!

Jo   Well, yes, I suppose . . .

Judith   On each page a picture of the toilet seat with the celebrity face inside it. How many, Jo?

Jo   Well, no more than eight. I do have to write the captions as well.

Judith   Marvellous, and that's a lot of work for you . . . Now, timing, when do you think we could expect to see a first draft? Bearing in mind we want to target the Christmas market 1995 which means we're looking at

going to print in 1993 and *tempus fugit*, so therefore if
you can let us have something in by the end of next
year we would be eternally grateful . . . (*Pause.*) A
page? Maybe?

Jo   I could get a sentence to you. Oh no, wait, not a
sentence, probably the first letter will be written by
then.

Judith   That would be great because you see, until we get
something from you we actually have nothing to do in
the office. We've got nothing to do *at all* until you
give us something.

Jo   What will you do with the first letter?

Judith   Photocopy it, send it round, discuss it and have lunch.

Jo   You realise it will be a capital letter, don't you?

Judith   Really? I'm not sure our budget has projected for
that.

Jo   Yes, and not only that, I'll be wanting to use another
seven Capitals and fourteen exclamation marks in this
book.

Judith   If you really want them, Jo, you can have them. Now,
the book launch . . .

Jo   Oh yes, I want tickets for that as soon as possible.

Judith   Yes, but first we *must* organise a lunch to discuss the
launch . . . For instance, Juliette and Samantha have
hit on the wonderful idea of sending genuine toilet
seats to people as invitations, because you'd be certain
to turn up at *that* party wouldn't you, if a toilet seat
came through the post?

Jo   Definitely.

Judith Right, I think that's everything then . . . a *very*
            successful meeting, Sue, and you know I'm always
            here if you need me before our lunch on Friday.

Jo   Here? You mean in the office?

Judith No, here, in this restaurant. Always here – Julian,
            poppet, we're ready to order at last. Oh, one last
            thing, Jo. Do you think pop-up is something you
            could incorporate in *Rock Stars and Their Toilet Seats*?
            I've got a mock-up to show you. (*Produces a pop-up
            toilet seat with Jane Asher's face inside toilet.*) Obviously
            it won't be Jane Asher really, it was just the only
            picture we had in the office; it will be Bob Geldof.

Jo   I think it's great. Can I say one thing. We should call
            it *Plop-Up*.

            They shake hands.

Judith You're worth every penny.